Lo-Fi + Mash-Ups

Warning

This is just some fiction,
This is just a piece of art,
This is just some imagination,
This is a collection of some dreams,
This is also a collection of hallucinations,
This has nothing to be called real,
There is no meaning in all this,
I am just a failed writer,
These are just words.

Still,
this is
a piece of
art.

Lo-Fi + Mash-Ups

A Journey of Continuance

Traveled by Amit

I Love you Tanya

This book should start with the mention of my loving, caring and funny wife, Tanya. I don't think that she considers herself funny, but yes she is funny too.

Her presence helps me to evolve, strive ahead, do some meaningful things in life and much more. She has been a constant support and constructive critic in my life.

This book is also a surprise for her and I hope she would like my creativity. So, I hope she finds this book interesting and finally acknowledge my creativity.

I love you Tanya.

Acknowledgments

First of all, I would like to thank you for showing a much necessary faith on this book. I wanted to say some more fancy stuff but you know what, you are already awesome.

Secondly, I thank people around me, family, friends, peers, elders, young, and everyone else I met or passed by who made this moment possible. Only because of you, I got the strength to continue writing and the book is finally published after an ebb and flow of eighteen years.

I must acknowledge the fact that writing a book was an amazing and exciting journey for me. I encourage everyone reading this book to write a book of their own. It will change the way you look at life.

Table of Contents

The content is on shuffle play x
no sections, no themes ....y
nothing ....z
Just random ideas ....a
put together for you to enjoy ....b

Never mind c
just read this book ....d
and you will i
get to know what's inside ii

"I am the wisest man alive, for I know one thing, and that is that I know nothing."

- Socrates, 470 - 399 BC, Athens

Preface

Lets talk about what you could get in this book. First of all don't mind the sarcasm, satire, philosophical anecdote or any useless ideas.

Let's live in this moment.

This book has evoked many emotions inside me and I am sure that you will also feel my emotional journey. Let me be a bit honest, there is nothing new or unique that is written in this book. You must have heard, seen or already read these ideas. I have just written what I thought was worth writing. So, if you buy this book and complaint about how bad this book is, the joke is on you. Did it become too dark a humour? (Fun Intended), please continue reading.

Last but not the least, if you find typos, grammatical mistakes, design flaws, lack of meaning or anything else, my humble apologies in advance. This is my first book, so please show some love. This book is meant to be like a bouquet of various emotions through different forms of expressions and I am sure a part in you would definitely like it.

So, let's get started.

Are You

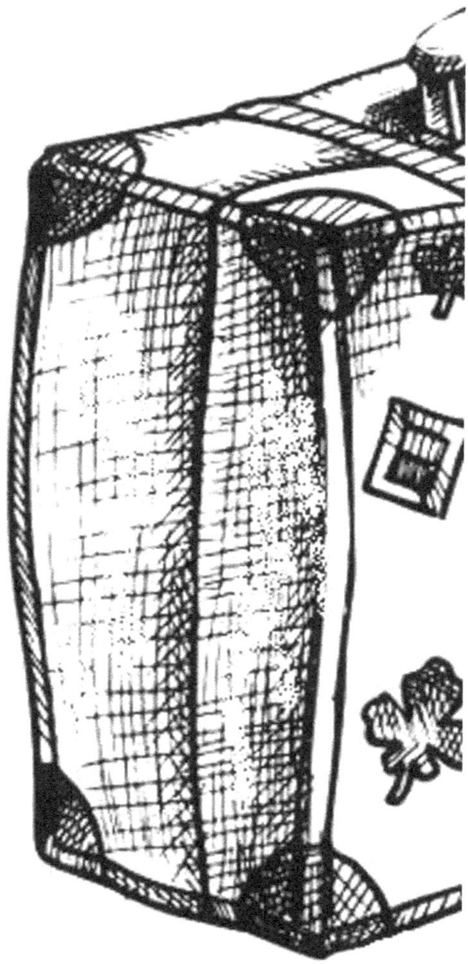

Ready?

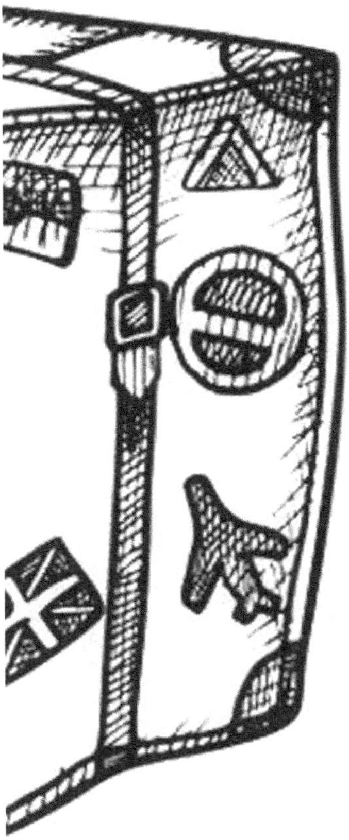

Playlist

(O) **Leaving On A Jet Plane** - John Denver (cover) | Reneé Dominique

(O) **Let Her Go** | Passenger

(O) **Shape of You** | Ed Sheeran

(O) **Cheap Thrills** | Sia

(O) **My Oh My** | Camila Cabello

(O) **Take Me Home, Country Roads** | John Denver

I will wait

I will wait for you...
I will see the sun shine furiously,
and clouds rain in anguish.

I will see the moon wax passionately,
and the moon wane in agony.

I will see the stars shine wildly,
and the stars shimmer in grief.

I will listen birds chirping all excited,
and birds fly away in fright.

I will see the flowers bloom zestfully,
and the flowers fade away in parts.

I will still wait for you.
I will see seasons change,
I will see rivers flow,
I will see mountains grow,
I will see oceans rise,
I will see the life disappear.

I will see all this submissively,
just to catch a glimpse of you.
I will still wait for you.

Rose

I am not bold enough to confess,
That, my heart plunges every time I see you.

Rose, you dwell in my mind like a verse,
But, my words fizzle out every time I talk to you.

The laughter we enjoy in cafes,
The gossips we pass on in washrooms,
The cigarette we share in parking lots,
All this, help me survive the world's unkindness,
At the end of the day,
I don't want to let go when I hug you.

Boys skip football game to get your glimpse,
To catch your attention they bring many gifts,
Some call you gorgeous, some say princess,
All this, make me crave for you immense,
It's not going to be easy to live without you,

Will I ever be able to tell you?
That, my heart whines every time I leave you.

Esclava

You think you own her,
because she said she loves you.
But, do you know...

She saw the world applaud her stunning
English recital in primary school.

She saw the world fall apart on her
first breakup in high school.

She made friends in college and saw
the world in rainbow colors.

She worked many jobs and somehow
managed to get a degree too.

You don't know that all this happened,
but today you think you own her,
because she said she loves you.

She walked many miles from work on
chilly nights to save some penny.

She couldn't even eat a sandwich in
the entire day when her stomach hurts.

She goes out of her way to get things done at work to prove she deserves the next promotion.

She is still fighting her depression since the car crash took her family away.

You don't know that all this happened,
but today you think you own her,
because she said she loves you.

Thank you.

I hope you are still reading.

Please continue.

Random Conversations

And life is walking slow and
fast on the streets,
talking to me
about my
life.

But, I don't know
if it's dawn
or dusk.

Cactus

Hello Cactus,

Did you brush your thorns deliberately,
When I first came to this desert?

I was just trying to look tough,
I haven't seen a plant like this before.
Someone said, it didn't rain here from decades,
I was surprised you have water inside.

I don't know what attracted me more,
The life inside you or
the way you wanted to take my life away?

Not many talk about your flowers,
Wow, it makes desert look so beautiful.
You said we can't be just friends,
I don't know where is this taking me?

I am not leaving this desert for some time,
It seems cactus,
You are the perfect partner to die with.

Your beloved,
Butterfly.

(English translation of next poem)

Storms knock every day at my door,
Not even the fear of death can silence me.

Yesterday, mother wrote in the letter,
Do not leave home in the morning hungry,
You have to fight the world,
Do not cover yourself with so much oppression.

Dad also seemed angry, wrote
Believe in your understanding,
But in this world, knowledge isn't well respected.

I think if I write a letter, what should I write in it,
I see fake characters of this city every day,
Have said many times, do not worry about me so much.

I will rise again tomorrow and fight again,
Not even the fear of death can silence me.

लड़ेंगे जी भर

तूफ़ान तो हर रोज़ दस्तक देते हैं हमारे दर,
हमें कहाँ चुप करा पायेगा अब मौत का डर.

कल माँ ने खत में लिखा था,
भूखे पेट सुबह घर से ना निकला कर
तेरी दुश्मनी जमाने से है,
खुद पे इतना जुल्म ना ढाया कर.

पिताजी भी नाराज़ से लग रहे थे, लिखा है
माना तेरी समझ में इल्म है बहुत
मगर इस जहाँ में किसको है नेकी की कदर.

सोचता हूँ, के खत लिखूं तो उसमे क्या लिखूं
हमें रोज़ दिखते हैं इस शहर के जाली किरदार,
कई बार कह दिया है, मत किया करो मेरी
इतनी फिकर.

हम कल फिर उठेंगे और फिर लड़ेंगे जी भर
हमें कहाँ चुप करा पायेगा अब मौत का डर.

God, I am upset with you

Yes, I am upset with you.

Are you upset with me,
because I don't kneel
in front of you?

You don't care for me,
because now I don't remember
the things I said to you?

You aren't generous to me,
because its difficult to
measure the prosperity
given to the world by you?

Are you invisible to me,
because you have already
left the world created by you?

It's not just about me,
many humans suffer
the unfair practices
followed by you.

Animals don't have the disparity,
that humans face.

If humans created all this
chaos,

Why is this allowed by you?

Yes, I am upset with you.

God, you need to prove,
that every day I lived
was worth bearing the pain,
given by you.

Bonita

I admire the warmth of you.

I admire the struggles you conquered,
I admire the knowledge you acquired,
I admire the warmth of you.

I saw you are mother, sister, daughter, lover
and much more to this world.
I saw you come early than sun
and left after the moon to make the ends meet.
I admire the warmth of you.

I think you could blossom like a flower,
I think you could also be stronger than a rock,
I know that you don't need me,
But, I still admire the warmth of you.

" Man is defined as a human being and a woman as a female - whenever she behaves as a human being she is said to imitate the male. "

- Simone de Beauvoir, 1908 - 1986, Paris

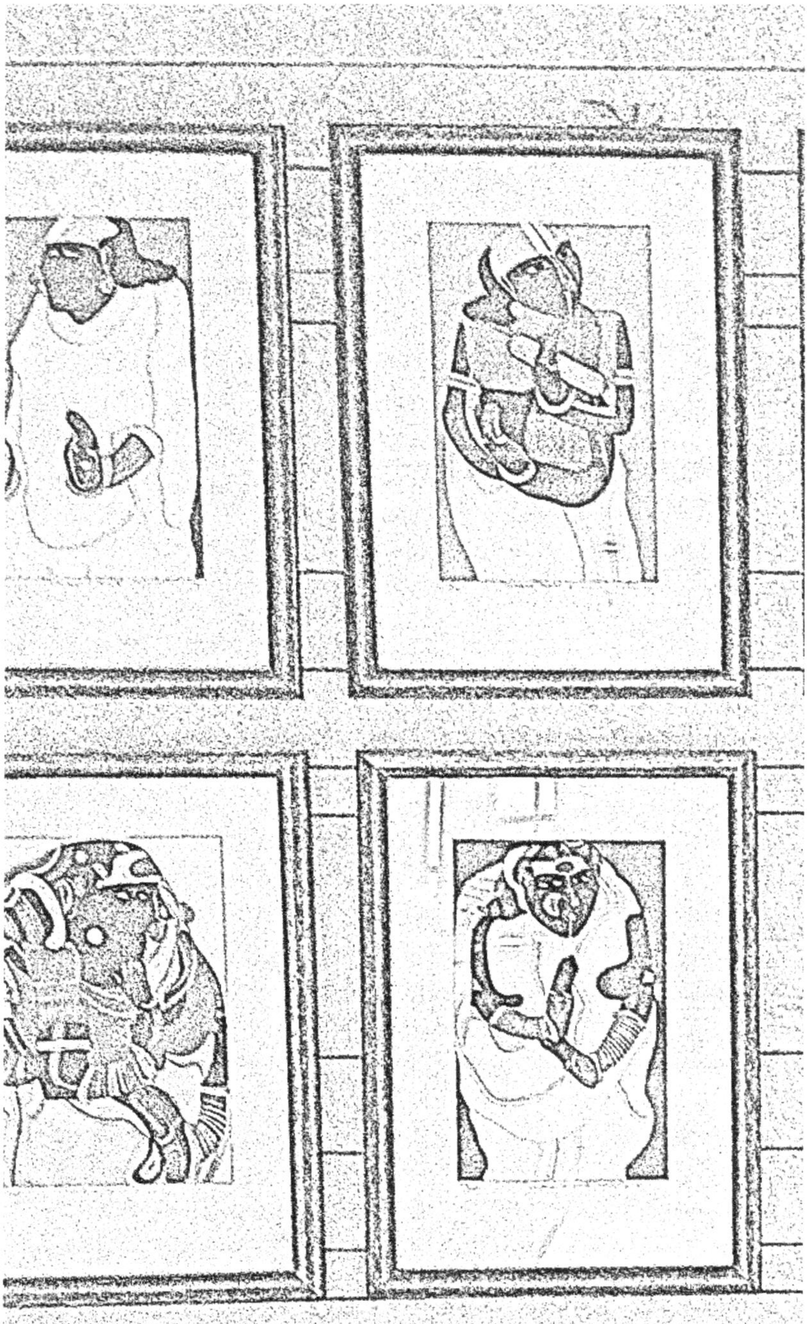

Nice

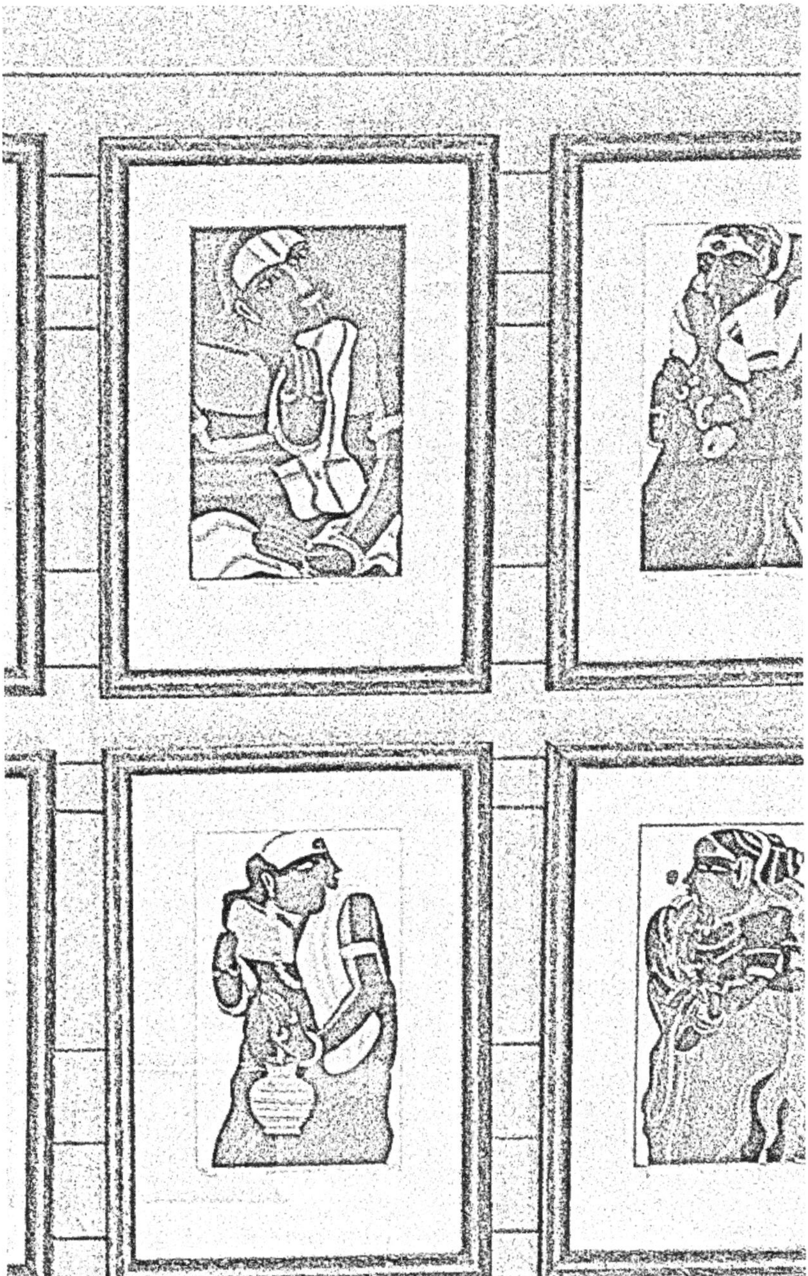

isn't It?

I try

I try,
Just to fill the void
of nothingness in my life.
The void itself is filled
with nothingness and everything else.

I try and cry,
Just to fill the void
of life in my existence.
The void itself is filled
with dead desires inside.

I cry and die,
Just to fill the void
of existence in my dreams.
The void itself is filled
with pure evil in every breath.

I die and say goodbye,
Just to keep moving,
Keep moving to stay alive
with never-ending process
of filling the void.

Yes, I try everyday.

Bella

Yes Bella, you are beautiful.

Yea Bella, you are wonderful.

Yes Bella, you have
changed my
world.

Yes Bella, you have
my soul
entangled.

Yes Bella, you left
but
I have you in me.

Yes Bella, we will meet again,
I am hopeful.

And, you will always be
wonderful.

Random Conversations

We hope, so we face disappointments.

But if not for hope, why the roses
on the bushes are here for?

They say, roses were born when
Adonis' blood hit the
ground.

Roses are the symbol
of rebirth and
hope.

Set About

She had a dream to find true love one day,

Set about like a cascade on a sunny day.
Happy to walk away without any delay,
To the comfort of manor she said "nay",
Set about on a journey to find "bae".

Experiencing the new world everyday,
Has fallen in love for the morning ray,
Learning new skills to write on Résumé,
Not missing the quiet of her town pathway,
Set about on a journey to find "bae".

She is no more a prey,
Decided to fight the world and not just pray,
The new confidence is no less than slay,
She said "now I want to play",
who is there to criticise the maverick, "cliché"?
She has realised, She is her own "bae",

Set about like a cascade on a sunny day.

(English translation of next poem)

I liberated myself by writing something,
Otherwise it was difficult to live with the burden of your thoughts.

Everyday I wait for your letter,
Every evening I asked god for your company.

There are so many stars in your party today,
Do people only praise your beauty
Or has anyone asked your heartache?

It must be my fault,
Otherwise, you have never been so bad to someone.

I freed myself by writing this much,
Otherwise, the burden of my loyalty had made it difficult to live.

वफ़ा

कुछ लिख के आजाद कर दिया खुद को हमने,
वरना जीना मुश्किल कर दिया था, तेरे ख्यालों के बोझ ने.

हर रोज़ तेरे खत का इंतज़ार किया है हमने,
हर शाम तेरा दीदार खुदा से माँगा है हमने.

तेरी महफ़िल में आज सितारों का रेला है,
ये सुना है हमने.
सिर्फ हुस्न की तारीफ़ लोग करते हैं,
या तेरे दिल का दर्द भी पूछा है किसी ने?

हमारा कसूर है,
वफ़ा में कुछ कमी रखी होगी हमने.
वरना बेवफाई इतनी शिद्दत से कब निभाई है तुमने.

इतना लिख के आजाद कर दिया खुद को हमने,
वरना जीना मुश्किल कर दिया था, मेरी वफ़ा के बोझ ने.

Gold-Digger

All she wanted was a fishing trip that
reminds her of her father.
All she wanted was a walk to church that
reminds her of her mother.

But you told everyone "she is a Gold-Digger".

All she wanted was a bicycle run that
reminds her of her brother.
All She wanted was a pillow fight that
reminds her of her sister.

But you told everyone "she is a Gold-Digger".

She kept looking at the photo album that
reminds her of her grandmother.
She kept that old watch that reminds
her of her grandfather.

But you told everyone "she is a Gold-Digger".

She still remembers the first McD date,
when you only had enough money
for fries & burger.
She still thinks of you, when people call
her world's best author.
But you told everyone "she is a Gold-Digger".

Together

He said:
Why I see this as a war?
When there is no blood.

Why you say this is love?
When there is no passion.

Are we in this together?

She replied:
Even if you are far away, I can still feel
your heartbeat.

Please

We Are Hungry

Heaven is Empty

No one in this world has been
away from sins.

We think we are better
than others.

We find the evil in others
and saint inside us.

We love to find fault
in our neighbours.

We are just living a life
full of illusions.

Heaven is empty,
all of us has blood
on our hands.

The Heaviest Thing

The heaviest thing
pressing your heart,
won't be regret but
Guilt.

Trust me, you have
no way to be at peace.

Everyone I met today,
was suffering because of
the unbearable pain of
life.

Only few of them know this.

The Heaviest thing
is to know this.

(English transaltion of next poem)

You kept quiet on everything.
I kept fumbling but it was hard,
To understand the pain in your silence

You were lost somewhere, you kept silence,
I was waiting, but didn't know that
It will be difficult for you to return.

Sometimes you said something,
I restlessly kept asking
And you ignored questions.

It will be difficult to forget your style of speech.

मुश्क़िल

तेरा कुछ ना कहना, हर बात पे चुप रहना.
हम अलफ़ाज़ टटोलते रहे लेकिन मुश्क़िल था,
तेरी ख़ामोशी में दर्द समझ पाना.

तेरा गुम हो जाना, कहीं चुप चाप खो जाना,
हम पलकें बिछाये बैठे रहे, मालूम नहीं था के,
मुश्क़िल होगा तेरा लौट के वापस आ पाना.

तेरा कभी कभी कुछ कहना,
हम बेचैन हो कर पूछते रहे
और तेरा सवालों को नज़रअंदाज़
कर आगे बढ़ जाना.

अब मुश्क़िल होगा, तेरे अंदाज़े बयां को भुला पाना.

I want to know you

I want to know more about you.
Everything
Every pain you bear
Everything you care
Every tear you shed
Every laugh you laughed
Every dream you dreamed
Every hope you hoped

We talk everyday
But I don't know anything about you.

My Conscious

I left to save Leningrad, but
Your good bye held my conscious back.

Trembling sound of your voice,
Your Eyes bathed in tears,
The dejection on your face,
You hugged me with distress,
You said good bye with such a grace,
That, my conscious never reached the army base.

I left to save Leningrad, but
Your good bye held my conscious back.

For too long people here lived in sickness,
They could do anything to save loved ones,
Even peel of a potato is considered marvellous,
The enemy is shouting loud at the gates,
I never saw battle so fierce,
We fought day and night and reached solace.

I came back saving Leningrad, but
The aftermath held my conscious back.

I don't know what to do with my own conscious.

All I Need

All I need is your love tonight.

All I need is, you tell me "how gorgeous am I ?"
But, I don't want you to fake.

I want you to show me how you truly feel,
I want you to tell me that you don't think
of anyone else,
I want you to bring me gifts
that matter to me.

I want you to make me feel special,
But, I want you to give me my space also.
All i need is your love tonight.

I want you to respect me,
I want you to also care for me,
I want you to give me physical pleasure,
But, I don't want you to think
that I am an object.
All I need is your love tonight.

I want you to listen to me patiently,
I want you to guide me
but not handhold me.
All I need is, just your love for entire life.

Failure of a Great Mind

The journey to become a great mind,
brings the failure alongside.

The path to know something rare,
makes the loneliness appear.

The road to know life's absurdity,
makes it difficult to handle reality.

The streets to know geo-political nexus,
makes me question the existence.

The alley to know generosity,
can never kill world's monstrosity.

Every step of consciousness
in my mind,
brings pain to my heart alongside.

The journey to become a great mind,
brings the failure alongside.

What?

I love you.

You're probably thinking "You don't even know me".

But, if people can hate for no reason, I can love.

- Unknown

Bygone

I thought all my problems will be bygone
as I will grow up, but

With the happiness of salary credit in account,
Bygone the lazy afternoon sibling rivalries.

With the drive to live in a big city,
Bygone the sanctuary of mother's endless love.

With the hunger to accomplish
most difficult assignment,
Bygone the knowledge of
father's inspiring war stories.

With the lust to drink wine
in a fancy restaurant,
Bygone the delight of Sunday picnics.

With the urge of an exquisite social life,
Bygone the comfort of
morning sunshine on the porch.

I think, the life is like a jigsaw puzzle to solve,
Bygone all my happiness and
the desire to grow up.

(English translation of next poem)

There is no effect of prayers
anymore.

You are happy far away,
We are sitting in loneliness.

Even if you forget me,
I will remember you in my prayers.

I know,
There is no effect of prayers
anymore.

दुआ

ना दुआओं मे असर है,
ना बद्दुआओं मे.

तू कहीं दूर खुश है,
हम बैठे हैं तन्हाईयों मे.

चाहे वो भुला भी दे हमें,
शामिल रहेगा हमारी दुआओं मे.

मालूम है, ना दुआओं मे असर है,
ना बद्दुआओं मे.

Why do I still love you?

All I get is pain but, why do I
still love you?

We built this house with passion,
Now, why it looks like a hotel to you?

You cared for every single need of me,
Now, why it feels like a trivial task to
you?

You listened to me for hours in cold
winter nights,
Now, why it sounds like a
lame story to you?

You told everyone that we are
made for each other,
Now, why it is so difficult
to see in my eyes to you?

I know, we have split roads
ahead of us,

I know, all I have is bittersweet
memory of us,
But, I will still love you.

I will Pray for You

Oh Maria,
I don't believe in god,
but, I will still
pray for you.

You are fighting
so strong,
You are facing all
on your own,
No one knows
You live in pain.

The world was never
nice to you.
I could be the friend
who will listen
to you.
But, you never let
me draw near
to you.

Oh Maria,
I don't believe in god,
least I can do,
I will pray for you.

Let's Cry

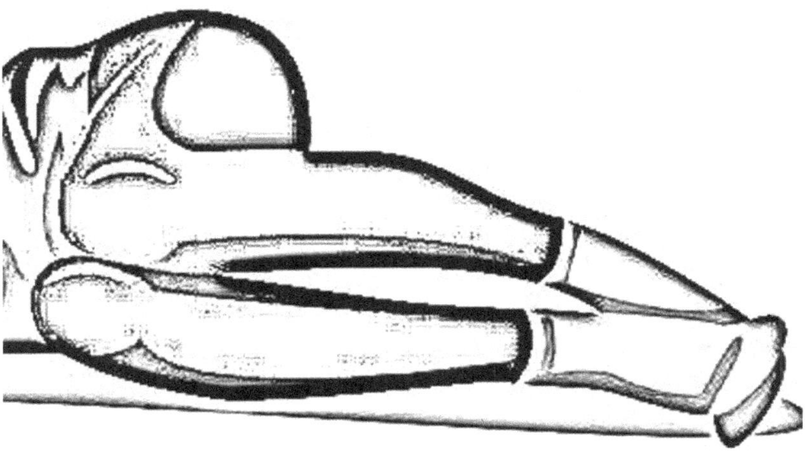

Together

" You will never be happy if you continue to search for what happiness consist of. You will never live if you are looking for the meaning of life. "

- Albert Camus, 1913 - 1960, France

If I Tell You

If I tell you, I think of you,
Will you make fun of me?

If I tell you, I miss you,
Will you believe in me?

If I tell you, I admire you,
Will you care to guide me?

If I tell you, I cooked for you,
Will you bother to eat with me?

If I tell you, I pray for you,
Will you trust the human in me?

If I tell you, I want to see you,
Will you still be mad at me?

If I tell you, I have & will always love you,
Won't you hear the plea presented by me?

Evil Me

I wished something at the Shooting star.
But, I had instant regret.

Will I still be considered Evil?

I wished for your company,
that could destroy my life's journey.

But, I don't want any one to be hurt.

Will I still be considered Evil?

I wished, I could give
you some love that you
have never received.

But, I don't want to take away love from
others in need.

Will I still be considered Evil?

I want to be with you,
it's the simplest thing,
Which could complicate everything.

Let me be considered Evil.

Thank you.

You have come too far.
I am sure you are loving this.
If not, just remember you haven't come
this far, to just, come this far.
Please continue.

(English translation of next poem, very bad but this is what we have, fun intended)

Clothes were dry, still wet,
It seems to rain.

Everything was fine, then the lovers are scattered,
The storm appeared.

We walked together for a few moments, have become lonely again,
There seems to be an interesting twist.

Hearts began to dream, then started living in pain,
Seems cheated.

Clothes were dry, still wet,
It seems to rain.

Someone knocked he door.
Feelings are growing in the heart,
Now comes the season of heartbreak.

लगता है

कपड़े सूख गए थे, फिर भीग गए हैं,
बारिश हुई लगता है.

सब संभल गया था, फिर आशियाने बिखर गए हैं,
तूफ़ान आया लगता है.

हम कुछ पल साथ चले थे, फिरसे तनहा हो गए हैं,
कोई दिलचस्प मोड़ आया लगता है.

दिल सपने पिरोने लगा था, फिर दर्द में जीने लगे हैं,
धोखा मिला लगता है.

कपड़े सूख गए थे, फिर भीग गए हैं,
बारिश हुई लगता है.

दस्तक हुई दर पे कोई
दिल में अरमान पनपने लगे हैं
फिर दिल टूटने का मौसम आया लगता है.

Heart-Eater

My heart has dreams to see the world,
My heart has desires to fly like a bird,
My heart has wishes to be heard,
My heart has images of love so absurd,
My heart has happiness deep down retard,
My heart has pain uncured,
My heart lost the battle with my mind,
My heart is scared,
I know you will eat it alive, but
Oh Heart-eater, I bring to you my heart.

My soul has lived so far ignored,
My soul never admired a reward,
My soul sometimes believed in god,
My soul is tangled in your thoughts like a cord,
My soul also sounds for you like a guitar chord,

I know you will eat it alive, but
Oh Heart-eater, I bring to you my soul.

Sorry, I can't write today. I have to study for exams.

Random Conversations

If it's autumn here,
it must be spring
somewhere.

The sun is walking
away to light
up other
worlds.

The sun will come
back with
memories
of those
worlds.

Let's Meet

Let's come together to end this nightmare.

We have been living on distant ends,
Let's meet in the middle of nowhere.

Things were difficult for both of us,
We didn't know the life is unfair.

Let's come together to end this nightmare.

The life is an endless race,
But, we will find our peace somewhere.

We have been living in despair,
Let's give us in each other's care.

Let's come together to end this nightmare.

(English translation of next poem, again its bad)

Today, I have visited your city,
have fallen in love with you again.
I didn't find you, but...

Your blissful laughters have been heard in every street,
Tasted sharpness of your words in the cuisine,
Your careless walk was visible in the flowing waterfalls,
Your unique style was in the carvings of the Taj Mahal.
I didn't find you but fallen in love with you again.

Today, I have visited your city,
have fallen in love with you again.
I didn't find you, but...

The depths of your eyes was in that lake,
The scent of your body was in a famous garden,
Your face was visible in the rays of the rising sun,
Your wise words were all over the library.

I prayed for you in every temple and mosque.
I knew there's no point, but I waited for you at the city center.

Today, I have visited your city,
I didn't find you, but...
have fallen in love with you again.

शहर

आज तेरे शहर से हो के आये हैं,
एक बार फिर इश्क़ करके आये हैं,
तुझपे थोड़ा और मरके आये हैं.

हमें तू तो ना मिला लेकिन,

तेरी खिलखिलाती हन्सी हर गली में सुन के आये हैं,
तेरी ज़ुबां का तीखापन चाट-पाप्डी में चख के आये हैं,
तेरी अल्हड चाल बहते झरनों में देख के आये हैं,
तेरी अनोखी अदाएँ ताज की नक्काशियों में
महसूस कर के आये हैं.

हमें तू तो ना मिला लेकिन,
तुझपे थोड़ा और मरके आये हैं.

आज तेरे शहर से हो के आये हैं,
एक बार फिर इश्क़ करके आये हैं,
तुझपे थोड़ा और मरके आये हैं,

हमें तू तो ना मिला लेकिन,

तेरी आँखों की गहराई उस झील में नाप के आये हैं,
तेरे बदन की खुशबू एक मशहूर बगीचे में ढून्ढ के आये हैं,
तेरे चहरे का नूर उगते सूरज की किरनों में देख के आये हैं,
तेरी समझदारी भरी बातें कुतुब खाने में पढ के आये हैं.

हर मंदिर और मस्जिद में तेरी सलामती की दुआ माँग के आये हैं,
झूठे ही सही,
तेरे शहर के चौराहे पे तुझसे मिल्ने का इन्तेज़ार भी करके आये हैं.

आज तेरे शहर से हो के आये हैं,
हमें तू तो ना मिला लेकिन,
एक बार फिर इश्क़ करके आये हैं,
तुझपे थोड़ा और मरके आये हैं.

Where are We Going?

This is not an ethics class. Let's see ourselves as a conscious animal. Yes, I said animal, because we are technically terrestrial animals. The idea is, we have gained more conscious than other animals and started calling ourselves "humans".

What I want to talk about, our volatile emotions that are the gift of evolution to us, stronger than any other animal. Can we talk about it more openly? Like, can we be happy not being ambitious to achieve something? Can we not be part of the party lover herd and still be relevant to the world?

Can we be a human, who doesn't want to harm other human because of our own hatred for others? Can we not expect everyone to be same? and not treat them differently based on gender, color, caste, creed, race, special abilities, weight, height and everything else? Is idea of diversity to lame for today's world?

Last, but not the least, isn't religion needs to be practiced in privacy ? As a society can we be religion agnostic? I think, it's high time in our evolution that we stop giving religion the undue respect and let food be the religion. Let's focus on food and feed people with love also.

Let's spread the love, be in love, share the love.

Tomorrow

Every day I grow old.

I won't look
this better tomorrow,
I won't feel
this better tomorrow.

Every day I grow old
to realize,
that I have been
lucky enough
to come this road,
and witness
many mysteries
unfold.

I will feel
the gratitude tomorrow,
I will surely look
for new mysteries
tomorrow.

Every day I grow old,
in search of
a new tomorrow.

Human Sacrifice

She goes out to earn the bread everyday,
She goes out...
With a smile on her face everyday,
And holding pain in her heart everyday,

She says, it is a ritual of life.
I say, it is a Human sacrifice.

She comes back and feeds the family everyday,
She comes back...
With tears in her eyes everyday,
And bruises in her soul everyday,

She says, it is a ritual of life.
I say, it is a Human sacrifice.

She leave her comfort zone too often,
She leave her comfort zone...
To make this world a better place for everyone,
And without telling her real story to anyone,

She says, it is a ritual of life.
I say, it is a Human sacrifice.

Letter to Myself at 15

Hello Amit,

I am writing this letter from future. I know, you would read this letter and still do whatever you think is right. You have always done this and trust me, you will always do this. So, why am I even writing this letter to you? It's not you, it's me (Humour intended)

I must tell you that, things will may or may not turn out to be the way you want them to be. You will face more failures than success, you will be more misunderstood than understood, people won't appreciate you the way you want. But, that's not the end. There is no end, don't try to outrun the present and find what's in the womb of future every second.

Learn how to relax. You do things far better than the people around you. Just trust yourself and don't be worried about your marksheets, job appraisals, promotions and what not. Keep doing whatever you are doing, you can't do better than this. Things will unfold and everything will be the way it is supposed to be.

Stop worrying and stop comparing yourself with others. That's it, do whatever you want.

See you in future.

"Nothing has such power to broaden the mind as the ability to investigate systematically and truly all that comes under thy observation in life."

- Marcus Aurelius, 121 - 180, Rome

I will see you tomorrow, said no Dog ever.

(English translation for next poem)

Today, the news of your departure came,
It's like a storm is brewing in my heart.

I suppose, I wasn't important at all for you,
To tell your the truth, I came to live with your words.

World found your words crooked,
We relieved from them and
We learned to walk in trouble.

Today, the news of your departure came,
It's like a storm is brewing in my heart.

राहत

आज तेरे जाने की खबर परिन्दा लाया,
तो जैसे दिल के एक कोने में कोइ तूफान आया.

माना हम कुछ नहीं थे तेरे लिये,
सच कहें तेरी बातों से हमें जीना आया.

तेरे अल्फ़ाज़ जमाने को टेढे लगे,
हमने उन्हीं से राहत पाई और
हमें मुसीबत में भी चलना आया.

आज तेरे जाने की खबर परिन्दा लाया,
तो जैसे दिल के एक कोने में कोइ तूफान आया.

Playlist

(0) **Six Feet Under** | Sofar Los Angeles | Billie Eilish

(0) **Wada Na Tod** | Dil Tujhko Diya | Lata Mangeshkar

(0) **Genesis** | Daniela Andrade

(0) **Stand By Me** | Ben E. King

(0) **Put Your Hand On My Shoulder** | Paul Anka

(0) **Ain't No Sunshine** | Bill Wither

(0) **Mere Mehboob** | Mr. X in Bombay | Kishore Kumar

A Day at a Time

Let's fight a day at a time ,
There is so much of chaos around,
We have seen forts falling on ground,
There are enemies faces frowned,
We have to make our soul proud.

Let's fight a day at a time,
Everyone is fighting inner wars,
We should not make this anymore sour,
If we need to, let's ignore,
only love can end this war.

Let's fight a day at a time.

Why did You Come Here?

I haven't seen humans here,
from long long time,
How did you just appear,
out of nothingness?
Did you come here,
along the river valley?
or you reached here,
climbing the mountains high?
Are more humans alive there,
from the place you came here?

You didn't look surprised to reach this wilderness,
How did you know so much about this place?
Why didn't you ever care to answer my questions?
Still, why there was so much love inside you,
Did you know my life has never been so blessed?
My inner scars were melting like a glacier,
Was there even a reason for you to come here?

I woke up this morning,
but haven't found you beside me.
Did you leave or you still around me?
It can't be a dream, do you agree?
Or am I hallucinating on the eclipse?
At least I have some new memories.
No one told me, love isn't friendly to peace.

Say Yes

Say Yes, and give someone,
a ray of hope today.

Things are difficult for you,
but you can still help anyway.
When you said,
"I am sorry I can't help you today"
do you know, they felt tear away?

They know, may be no one will help,
they still come and pray.
When you said,
"I don't like to step out on a rainy day"
do you know, they thought of
giving their life away?

Why don't we help each other?
Why don't we give people a ray of hope
to live for one more day?
Why don't we say "Yes, come my way"?

(English translation of next poem)

I might die without you,
But some breaths have been saved for you.

I consoled my heart to live without you,
For every pain I wrote a new song.

Finding your essence in books,
Thousands of stories have been kept for you.

Your thoughts surrounded me every moment,
Even if I am atheist, i pray for you.

This heartache is meaningless,
Will die to just listen to your voice,
Come and destroy me,
Some breaths have been saved for you.

तुम्हारे लिए

मर ना जाएँ कहीं बिन तुम्हारे,
मगर कुछ सांसें बचा रखी हैं लिए तुम्हारे.

दिल को समझाया कैसे बाद जाने के तुम्हारे,
हर दर्द को जैसे एक नया नगमा बनाया लिए तुम्हारे.

किताबों में रोज अक्ष ढूंढे तुम्हारे,
हज़ारों किस्से रट रखे हैं लिए तुम्हारे.

ख्यालों ने हर पल घेर रखा था तुम्हारे,
काफिर होके भी बस दुआ मांगी लिए तुम्हारे.

हाले-गम हमारा बेमाएने है इस कदर
के मर ही जाएंगे अल्फ़ाज़ों से तुम्हारे,
चलो आकर तबाह ही कारदो,
जो सांसें बचा रखी हैं लिए तुम्हारे.

You killed me

You killed me,
After you said,
You have respect for me.
For my own happiness,
I believe,
You always loved me.

You stopped me
to listen one more song with me.
You said you love
the philosophy with me.
You said you don't want
gifts from me.
You shared
your pain
with me.

I am happy,
for your own happiness
you killed me,

after you said,
You have respect for me.

But, I still believe,
You always love me.

Thank you.

Now, I can say that you are loving this.
You know it, the book will get more interesting now.
If you are reading non-stop, better take a break.

Cheers!

Random Conversation

It's high time you get serious about life.
(Fun Intended)

Tell Me a Sweet Lie

Tell me a sweet lie,
that you will come
to see me,
before I die.

Tell me a sweet lie,
that you will never
forget me,
even if you
never loved me.

Tell me a sweet lie,
that you will always
smile,
and will never
cry.

(English translation of next poem)

Tell me what do you do with my letters.
Do you keep them close to you heart or you sleep
peacefully by burning them?

The city was yearning for a drop of rain,
I prayed first you get wet in the rain, we can wait.

There was not a single answer to millions of my
questions.
Tell me what do you do with my letters?
You do not keep them close to your heart,
Do you submerge them in river?

I wrote every word from heart,
I wrote some, kept some in the heart.

Once I thought that you have changed the house,
The postman said that you are still happy at the old
address.

Anyways, everything is fine, but what do you do with
the letters in which the verses are sent?
You burn them or you are bury them somewhere?

खत

बता दो हमारे खतों का क्या करते हो तुम.
दिल से लगा के रखते हो या जला के चैन से सो जाते हो तुम?

बूँद बूँद को तरस रहा था शहर हमारा,
तुम्हारी ख़ुशी के लिए खुदा से दुआ की, के हम इंतज़ार कर
लेंगे, पहले बारिश में जी भर के भीग लो तुम.

हमारे लाखों सवालों का एक भी जवाब न आया,
बता दो हमारे खतों का क्या करते हो तुम?
दिल से लगा के तो नहीं रखते हो तुम,
क्या जगजीत की तरह गंगा में बहा देते हो तुम.

हर लफ़्ज़ दिल की सियाही से लिखे हमने,
कुछ लिखे, कुछ दिल में ही छुपा रखे हैं हमने.

एक बार हमे लगा के घर तो नहीं बदल दिया तुमने,
डाकिये ने कहा के पुराने पते पे ही खुशहाल हो तुम.

चलो बाकी सब ठीक है, लेकिन जिन खतों में आयतें लिख के
भेजी हैं, उनका क्या करते हो तुम?
उन्हें जला देते हो या कहीं दफना आये हो तुम?

Possibly

Of all possible evil,
I find the most dangerous in my head.

Of all possible virtues,
I find the most valuable in my conscious.

Of all possible pain,
I find the most striking in my heart.

Of all possible comforts,
I find the most soothing in my creativity.

Of all possible fears,
I find the most terror in my inaction.

Of all possible disasters,
I find the most destructing in my anger.

Of all possible wars,
I find the most destructing in my dilemma.

Of all possible disgusts,
I find the most repelling in my ignorance.

Of all possible warfare,
I find the most conquering in my writing.

But, of all possible happiness,
I find the most important nowhere.

A Beautiful Pain

I looked at your picture today to think about, why on this earth I fall in love with you?

I don't know what makes you happy or sad. I don't know what hurts you or excites you. We had some random conversations few times, that's it. I don't even know your full name. You never told me that what kind of food would you like to eat or where do you wanna go for a vacation this summer.

May be, I told you a lot about me, my food taste, my music playlist, my mood swings, my depression and what not. I don't think, I have been so carefree around others from quite some time. I don't know, I have seen myself in such a light before.

Well, there are so many people who hate me without any reason, at least I think so. So, why can't I love you without any reason? And, how beautiful it is, that we may never be in the same place at the same time, but I would still love you beyond time and space.

I will hold this beautiful pain in my heart forever.

I Love You

I love you.

I love the feeling of being in love
with you.
I love to hear the voice
of you.
I love to smell the fragrance
of you.
I love the way
I look
at you.

I love you.

I love the pain of being in
love with you.

Wish I could tell you,
how much I
Love you.

Wish I could
tell you, to Love me,
the way I
Love you.

Random Conversation

Someone asked me "do you like traveling?"
I said "self awareness journey is what I like"
Haven't heard back from that person after that.

(English translation of next poem)

Every moment in my breath, you live like a perfume,
Because of you, I travel peacefully in troubled times.

I also know this, only for our happiness
You live far away,
So many storms you fight everyday on your own.

My only hope is to meet you,
But the dreams that were woven together,
I don't want them to be destroyed by coming there.

Every moment in my breath, you live like a perfume,

जुदाई

मेरी साँसों में हर पल इत्र सा तू रहता है,
तेरे होने से ही हाले-गर्दिश में मुसाफिर इत्मीनान से चलता है.

ये भी मालूम है हमें, हमारे मुस्तक़बिल के लिए ही
बहुत दूर तू रहता है,
अकेले ही जाने कितने तूफानों से तू रोज लड़ता है.

बस तुझसे मिलने की आरज़ू ही ज़हन में है हमारे,
लेकिन वहां आ जाने से वो तबाह न हो जाएँ
जो मिलके बुने थे ख्वाब हमने,
इस बात का डर हमे रोके रखता है.

मेरी साँसों में हर पल इत्र सा तू रहता है.

Nothing

Really, Nothing

Narrow Elevator

Life is a narrow elevator.

There are many floors in the building of life and the progression isn't linear. One day you are on 14th floor, next day you have to be on 119th floor. Day after that you are asked to come down to ground floor.

To save time, it is advised to take elevator and avoid stair-case. It is practical too. The problem is, elevator is very narrow. Not too many people can fit in at the same time. You have to wait for too long and even if you catch the elevator, the journey isn't comfortable.

You will meet so many people, who will advise you to be quick, jump the queue, be smart, be competitive or have a winning attitude. Who the hell am I to judge them? I only advise to listen to your favourite music, read books, talk to someone, pick a hobby, watch movies, go out with friends, show compassion or call your parents to tell them that you are struggling in life. If you don't like someone, may be avoid them. If you like someone, tell them.

Live your life like a human. Be a human. Enjoy the humour. Laugh at yourself. Spread the love.

Just remember, only hugs no drugs.

Now, why it feels like,
we never met before?

Very Random Conversation

The Beauty

The beauty of
our Heart is about
being insane,

It heals again
and again, to be
broken again.

The beauty of
our soul is about
being divine,

It follows the
path of compassion
even in bane.

The beauty of
our body is about
being unbroken,

It remains strong
even in storms
or rain.

The beauty of
our life is about
being nice to
everyone.

And give our
Love to people
around us
again and again.

To fall in
Love
again and again.

This is All I have

Did I give you more Love
than I should have?
Trust me, this isn't all I have,
But, this is all I can.

Did I give you just Love
nothing else that I should have?
I know, this isn't all you needed,
But, this is the only thing I have.

Did I give you more pain
than I should have?
I don't know, why I hurt you,
But, you are the only person I have.

Did I leave too early
than I should have?
I wasn't able to see you in pain,
But, this is all I can.

Yes, I will always
Love you more
than I should.

"In spite of everything, I still believe that people are really good at heart."

- Anne Frank, 1929 - 1945, Frankfurt

Try, May Be Not

"I cannot make you understand. I cannot make anyone understand what is happening inside me. I cannot even explain it to myself."

From "The Metamorphosis"
- Franz Kafka, 1883 - 1924, Austria

Solution To Your Every Problem, Almost

The theory of evolution by Charles Darwin is so interesting. Yes, I am talking about science again, and you may be disappointed that I am not giving you a spiritual answer here.

Anyways, human evolution was so rapid and self destructive, that most of our modern problems are caused by our own evolution. There are so many things we do because our monkey brain (humour intended) is still trying to survive. However, modern society has no place for vulnerability and true emotions. Thus, we are getting submerged in the sea of depression, anxiety and many other unusual problems.

I am not a specialist in human psychology, but I think this should be the most important discourse. Let's talk about our beliefs, thoughts, emotions and passions. We are not suppose to be a manufacturing line product output. The diversity is our strength.

Solution is in front of us.

Random Conversation

You don't become what you want to be,
but, you become what you do,
when you are becoming what you want.

Random Conversation

We didn't become atheist
without any reason,
We are made to lose faith.

Letter to Son at 9

Dear Adwit,

I am writing this letter for you to read, when you turn 9 or may be later, it's up to you. Anyways, why after 8, because I still remember my enthusiasm, self confidence and curiosity towards life when I was 9 years old.

I don't want you to do few things or avoid few other things or anything like that. But, what I want you to do, is believe in science, philosophy, art, music and everything else, but first learn about everything. Don't jump into conclusions. Think about things carefully. Knowledge is the most important thing.

Is there a god or not? Will aliens attack us? What the hell did Dali painted? or Why Mahatma Gandhi sacrificed his life for a country? These questions are worth, all of them. Don't worry about finding all the answers. But try your best.

You will find love, have heartbreaks, achieve success, and see failures. All this is unavoidable. There is nothing new in all this. Find your passion, find what you really want to do in life. Only that will be with you forever. I can write an entire book it seems.

Anyways, enjoy and don't forget to be humble.

Playlist

(O) **Wherever You Are** | Synecdoche Montauk

(O) **Chan Kithe Guzari Ayee Rat** | Surinder Kaur

(O) **(Everything I Do) I Do It For You** | Bryan Adams

(O) **Noor E Khuda** | My Name is Khan |Adnan Sami| Shreya Ghoshal

(O) **What A Wonderful World**|Louis Armstrong

(O) **Wish You Were Here** | Oink Floyd

(O) **Girls Like You** | Maroon 5

(English translation for next poem)

You understand by looking at the face, that
The storm is overflowing in my heart.
You know by listening to the voice,
How it is wreaking havoc on me?

You are the mother.
I know how many tears you hide,
And you give medicine to all my pain.
You know how to handle all this,
You are the mother, you understand everything.

Your prayers have effect,
I am alive,
Otherwise, the world is all against my life.

माँ

तू चेहरा देख के समझ जाती है,
के मेरे दिल में तूफ़ान उमड़ रहा है.
तू आवाज़ सुन के जान जाती है,
के मुझपे कैसा कहर बरप रहा है.

तू माँ है.
जाने कितने आंसूं तू छुपा लेती है,
और मेरे हर दर्द को तू दवा देती है.
जाने कैसे ये सब संभाल लेती है,
तू माँ है, तू सब समझ जाती है.

तेरी दुवाओं का असर है,
जिन्दा हैं हम,
हमे जमीदोज़ करने की
वरना जमाने ने कसार कहाँ रखी है.

The Truth of Sisyphus

Albert Camus wrote in his book "The Myth of Sisyphus" that "one must imagine Sisyphus happy". I think it was a much necessary optimism that we needed. For the readers, new to the Greek mythology, Sisyphus was punished by God to roll-up a huge bolder up the hill for eternity, because he cheated death again and again.

Albert Camus also suggested that we can consider this as a striking similarity to our daily never ending repetitive life. What I am adding to this is, let's not assume Sisyphus to be simply happy. Let's consider that he was happy, sad, frustrated, bored, excited and much more with his punishment. May be he also fell in love with the boulder and developed a love and hate relationship with it.

The truth is, Sisyphus was facing the same emotions that we face everyday, every second. We are that Sisyphus. The life is meaningless but our actions need not to be meaningless. There is nothing at the end of this rat race and we can still find our own walk in here.

And yes, I don't know the truth you are looking for, you need to find it yourself. By the way, I will discuss about it in my next book.

Thank You

WOW! We are here. The last page of the book. I was not sure that you will reach this far. I must appreciate your efforts to read the book. This book has helped me evolve a great deal, hope it was of some sense to you too.

Hope the collection of poems, monologues and random thoughts is equally enjoyable as the songs. Anyways, its great to be part of this journey with you.

Till we meet gain, stay strong, have fun, enjoy, stay humble, act gracefully, think about global warming (I said it). Most importantly, stay safe & don't hurt others, not even animals.

www.ingramcontent.com/pod-product-compliance
Lightning Source LLC
Chambersburg PA
CBHW062142160726
48282CB00027B/914
9789354264801